SUGAR DETOX FOR BEGINNERS

10-DAY MEAL PLAN

BY NATASHA BROWN

Presented by French Number Publishing
French Number Publishing is an independent publishing house headquartered in Paris, France with offices in North America, Europe, and Asia.
FN₀ is committed to connect the most promising writers to readers from all around the world. Together we aim to explore the most challenging issues on a large variety of topics that are of interest to the modern society.

FREE DOWNLOAD

YOUR FREE GIFT!
GET MORE FREE RECIPES IN 1 CLICK!

GET YOUR FREE RECIPES HERE:

www.frenchnumber.net/detox10

INTRODUCTION

DAY 1

DAY 2

DAY 3

DAY 4

DAY 5

INTRODUCTION

HOW SUGAR GOT ITS BAD REP...

In order to properly and effectively detox from "Bad" sugar, it is necessary to first understand what exactly sugar is, why your body needs it and why there are "Good" sugars and "Bad" sugars.

Basically, the three types of carbohydrates found in the human diet (sugar, starch and fiber) are all sugar. Simple sugars consist of one or two molecules of sugar, start to break down in the mouth, and because they are so quickly introduced to the bloodstream, cause a spike in blood sugar and make us feel temporarily energetic, followed soon after by a crash. Think of how you feel 15 minutes after eating that mid-afternoon candy bar and sugar-laced coffee, and you get the picture. Starch and fiber, on the other hand, are complex sugars because they are made from three to hundreds of sugar molecules, take longer to digest, enter the bloodstream more slowly and give us a more even, sustained form of energy.

Energy is good. Hence, naturally occurring sugar found in fruits, vegetables, beans, nuts and whole grains, eaten in moderation, is "Good" sugar. Sugar, when accompanied by vitamins, minerals, protein, phytochemicals and fiber, which slows down the absorption of sugar in the bloodstream, equals a steady, consistent energy for our bodies to consume and run well on. However, when sugar is gratuitously added to food during processing, cooking or at the table, it becomes a source of extra calories with no nutritional value or fiber to slow the energy down. This "added" sugar is the "Bad" sugar that coats ALL sugar with a bad reputation. This book is filled with recipes designed to eliminate and detox "Bad" sugars from your diet and body in under a month!

So why is sugar added to food if it's such a bad thing? Primarily, sugar is a cheap, effective flavour enhancer. It boosts and amplifies the taste and texture of foods, ranging from desserts and snacks to more surprising foods, such as soup, bread and most shocking of all, Low and FAT-FREE foods like yoghurt and frozen dinners!

An even more insidious "benefit" of adding sugar to food, is its addictive quality. Basically, the addition of simple sugars, i.e., easily broken-down and digested sugars into foods, starts a vicious cycle of energy spikes and crashes which result in cravings for more and more of this quick-fix energy. Ironically, the very foods chosen by people trying to lose extra weight end up packing the pounds on, as well as flooding the body and blood with tons of sugary energy that can't be processed quickly enough. The body has to do something with the excess, so it stores this energy, in the form of FAT. Eventually, this continuous onslaught of sugar throws entire systems of the body off, and like the sludge of old oil in a car, our bodies become increasingly clogged up and less able to function at optimal capacity.

THE BENEFITS OF SUGAR DETOX:

The following list of benefits gained when you embark on a 21 or 10-day "bad" sugar detox are not, as you will discover, limited to your general health. Eliminating foods that contain added sugar will have a profound impact on many levels of your life!

Weight Loss: Eating whole vs. "processed" foods with added sugar in moderation aids in better digestion, elimination and weight control

Cost Savings: Eating foods found on "the edges" of a grocery store, i.e., fresh produce, meat, fish and whole grains, rather than "convenience" foods found in the frozen aisle, can lower food bills.

Positive Role Modeling: Inspire your family, kids and friends to break the "Bad" sugar habit, and influence future generations!

Increase "Real" Energy: When you eat whole foods with natural sugar, you are controlling your source of healthy, consistent and even energy intake.

Eliminate Cravings: Stop the vicious cycle of ingesting junk food, experiencing energy spikes and crashes and repeating this negative behavior.

Streamline your Grocery List: Buying and consuming whole foods and ingredients for sugar detox recipes will simplify your shopping.

- Stop Feeling Tired: Because of the energy highs and lows of added sugar, you end up feeling sleepy and sluggish in the middle of the day.

- Regulate Digestion: Consuming meals made up of whole foods increases fiber intake and aids in digestion and elimination.

- Clearer Skin: Unclog your body inside and out!

- Gain a "Happy" Tummy: Detoxing "Bad" sugar can help eliminate bloating, gas and nausea.

- Even out Mood Swings: Sugar spikes can result in increased anxiety. Sugar crashes can result in increased depression. Sugar detox can help control both.

- Increased Mental Clarity: If you are controlling anxiety and depression, you'll have more time to think clearly.

- Sugar Awareness: Detoxing necessitates reading the ingredient panels in everything you purchase and eat. You will become increasingly aware of all the surprising places sugar lurks.

- Improved Sleep: It stands to reason if your stomach is more settled and your energy is more consistent you will end up sleeping longer and deeper.

- Adding Diversity to your Diet: When you detox from added sugar, you will end up having to eliminate many old standbys in your diet. The good news is you will discover new whole food taste treats you would never have tried.

TWENTY ONE OR TEN DAY MEAL PLAN OPTIONS:

I have published 2 books on sugar detox: a 21 day-option, based on the well-known theory that it takes 3 weeks to develop a new habit and fully commit to it; and a 10-day option for people who want faster results and are willing to experience more intense withdrawal symptoms. These options are both included because people are motivated by and respond to varied experiences. Rather than a "one-size-fits-all" approach, you will be given two time frames in which to detox.

21-day Habit Modification Plans work on the assumption that a three-week time frame gives your body and mind a generous amount of time to adjust to positive change without undue stress or deprivation. It's also a lot more reasonable to tell yourself that you can cut out the offending habit, or in this case, food source for 21 days, rather than go cold turkey and declare that you will NEVER eat sugar again for the rest of your life. After the initial 21 day period, your body and mind have had ample time to recalibrate to life without added sugar; cravings have gradually and easily been eliminated and you have a three week period of success to look back upon and continue to motivate yourself as you look forward to a "Good" sugar future. 21 days also give you time to honestly reflect upon how you've felt in the past in comparison to how you are feeling as you detox from added "bad" sugar. This type of observation and reflection resonates well with people who require gradual transitions and more time to acclimate to change, without diminishing the positive results.

The 10-day meal plan was designed for people who are motivated by "jumping into the deep end" and who become disengaged or unmotivated by a process or plan that takes too much time. This more intense program are for those of you who are frankly sick and tired of feeling sick and tired and want to experience faster results, including the effects of a more sudden withdrawal from added sugar. People are different and the discomfort of sudden withdrawal that might discourage people drawn to the 21-day option actually motivates other people who look at these physical symptoms as concrete proof that "Bad" sugar has had such a profound effect on their well-being!

Whoever you are and whether you opted for the 21 or 10-day meal plan, both have been carefully designed to give you positive results without complicated instructions, hard-to-find ingredients and time consuming recipes. Both offer a clear, detailed approach to eliminating "Bad" added sugar from your diet by introducing delicious recipes prepared with healthful whole food ingredients

THE "BAD" SUGAR DETOX MISSION

Sugar Detox was well-explained in by David Zinczenko who continues his twenty-year mission to help people live their happiest and healthiest lives, uncovering revolutionary new research that explains why you can't lose weight – and shows that it's not your fault! The true culprit is sugar – specifically added sugars – which food manufacturers sneak into almost everything we eat, from bread to cold cuts to yoghurt, peanut butter, pizza, and even "health foods".

Do you ever watch old movies or TV shows and watch in resentful wonder as slim, attractive all American families sit down to eat huge home-cooked meals, complete with desserts? What happened? It doesn't make sense, that 50 years later, with all of our education, scientific and technological advances and understanding about the benefit of proper nutrition and exercise we have become a nation full of obesity, diabetes and stress-related disease!

The research has been conducted and compiled and the results clearly show that a major culprit of our increasingly unhealthy society is the addition of sugar to almost EVERY processed food we buy and consume today!

According to the American Heart Association (AHA) the maximum amount of added sugar you should eat a day for men is 9 tsp, and for women 6 tsp With that in mind, here are just a few examples of tsp of added sugar in one serving of processed foods:

- One can of regular soda: 8 tsp sugar

- One chocolate bar: 5.75 tsp of sugar

- Froot Loops cereal: 10.5 tsp of sugar

- ½ cup pasta sauce: 3 tsp of sugar

- One serving instant oatmeal: between 3 and 4 tsp of sugar

- 1 tbsp of Ketchup: 1 tsp of sugar

From the examples above, it's easy to see how you could exceed your daily recommended allowance in one snack or a few ingredients in a typical meal.

Sugar is added to foods for many reasons; none of which are to benefit your wellbeing. It is added to baked goods as a preservative to keep them fresher longer, to keep jellies and jams from spoiling, to aid in the fermentation process in bread and alcohol and to improve the color of foods and drinks!

Another sneaky way that sugar is added to your foods, especially those you may be buying because they are "healthy" and/or "organic" and "natural", is by listing it by other names, such as; agave syrup, brown sugar, corn sweetener and corn syrup, fructose, glucose, honey, malt syrup, raw sugar or molasses.

No matter what it's added to or what it's called, in the fight against added sugar, it sometimes feels as if you simply can't win for losing. How can you be blamed for gaining weight and jeopardizing your health when you have been consuming food and drink that has been literally "laced" with tons of added sugar?

This book has been conceived and written as a concrete weapon in the battle of added "Bad" sugar. It is full of healthy, delicious recipes that use whole food ingredients free from added sugar and empty calories. By simply following the 21 or 10 day meal plans, you will transform your diet from one filled with hidden "bad" sugar, to a nutritionally dense and filling menu of meals composed of foods bursting with vitamins, minerals, and "good" sugar that will give you authentic energy, allowing you to experience renewed vigor and a sense of balanced well-being.

Armed with nutritionally sound knowledge you will view the typical supermarket with clear, open eyes. As you shop, you will bypass many old favorites and menu standbys, now that you understand how unhealthy they are for you and your loved ones. Instead you will choose simpler, whole foods with no added ingredients, secure in the knowledge that you know EXACTLY what you are putting in your recipes and, ultimately, into your body.

So often nowadays you read about how fat, lazy and inactive American adults and their children are. Yet, the media is crammed with the latest health and fitness crazes and billions of dollars are spent every year on sports equipment, gym memberships, diet programs and food plans. You can't help but wonder why none of this incredible effort, time and money isn't improving the statistics. Again, it comes down to the irrefutable fact, that we are literally eating our weight in added sugar and empty calories. And the destruction doesn't stop there. Frighteningly, the more of this nutritionally bankrupt food we consume; the more we crave it, ingesting it in larger and larger quantities, even when it has been marketed to us as "low" or "no-fat"! In any other environment, this hypocrisy would be viewed as a criminal offense and punished as a highly illegal and immoral act. Yet, when it comes to our health, our very wellbeing, we continue to consume this subtle but devastating poison.

The health benefits of eating whole foods and "good" sugars are only part of the good news. Once you are firmly positioned on the road to physical good health, your mental and emotional wellbeing will improve as well. As you regain energy and vigor you will be able to enjoy life and accomplish goals you had once given up as impossibilities. Your economic health will also improve, as you rely less on processed, convenience foods and meals, and more on freshly prepared ingredients. Your tastes will evolve too and you will find yourself reaching into the fruit bowl rather than scrambling for extra cash to fund the empty calories found in a vending machine, coffee shop or fast food restaurant.

It all comes down to the difference between living to eat and eating to live. The possibility that we have been sold, along with added "Bad" sugar, the empty promise that if you eat this processed, "convenience" food, you will somehow be given more time to enjoy your life, fuelled by the temporary jolt of sweetened energy is one we must face down once and for all before it defeats our health and happiness. Rather, if we relearn to eat the foods nature has always provided us, free from added sugar, we can detox ourselves from an addictive, unnecessary ingredient in a relatively short period of time. When you consider it took years and years of eating poorly to get us to such a perilous state of health, ten or twenty one days is a mere blip on the timeline of life!

Ending any sort of food addiction can be a daunting, even overwhelming challenge. Unlike smoking, or gambling or most any other addiction, you simply cannot quit food. This book has been written with that knowledge constantly in mind. Through the 21 or 10-day meal plans, you will be able to eliminate the one element; added "Bad" sugar, which has tainted the food you have been eating. Once the added sugar has been eliminated and healthy whole food sources with natural "good" sugar have replaced it, you will have the time you personally require, be it 21 or 10 days, to acclimate yourself to the benefits of this one change as well as to experience the positive changes you will soon see in your physical health, mental clarity and outlook, and continued general well-being. Food is not the enemy. Naturally occurring "Good" sugar founds in fruits, vegetables, protein, beans, and whole grains isn't either. Added "Bad" sugar, introduced to our food sources to falsely enhance flavor, preservation, aesthetic appeal, economic viability and an addictive nature is the true enemy. A needless, senseless enemy that when eradicated will open our minds and bodies to the potential gift of true, lasting health. All you need is the desire to rid yourself of an unconscious, unhealthy habit. This book and its delicious 21 or 10-day meal plans will provide the rest of the solution!

TROPICAL BREAKFAST SMOOTHIE

/ SERVES 2-3 GLASSES / PREPARATION TIME 7 MIN. / COOKING TIME 0 MIN. /

INGREDIENTS

3 passion fruits
1 chopped banana
1 peeled and chopped apple
300ml orange juice
    ice cubes

NUTRITION PER SERVING

CALORIES — 162   PROTEIN — 3   FIBER — 4
SUGARS — 1   FAT — 0

INSTRUCTIONS

1. Scoop out the pulp from the passion fruits into a blender and add the banana, apple and the orange juice.
2. Blend until the mixture becomes smooth.
3. Top with ice cubes and drink immediately.

GARDEN PASTA SALAD

/ SERVES 1 / PREPARATION TIME 10 MIN. / COOKING TIME 15 MIN. /

INGREDIENTS

1 package uncooked spiral pasta (16 ounces)
½ cup of finely sliced carrots
2 finely chopped stalks celery
½ cup green bell pepper (finely chopped)
½ cup of finely peeled and sliced cucumber
2 large diced tomatoes
¼ cups of chopped onion
2 bottles of Italian-styled salad dressing
½ cup of finely grated Parmesan cheese

NUTRITION PER SERVING

CALORIES — 389   PROTEIN — 14   FIBER — 0.3
SUGARS — 1.3   FAT — 14

INSTRUCTIONS

1. Cook the pasta in a large pot of boiling water until it turns tender.
2. Rinse the pasta under water and drain. Add the chopped carrots, celery, cucumber, green pepper, tomatoes, and onion together in a large bowl. Merge together the cooled pasta and vegetables.
3. Sprinkle the Italian dressing over mixture, add the Parmesan cheese and mix it thoroughly. Allow it to cool down for one hour before serving.

TIP
Be on the lookout for Parmesan that contains vegetarian or microbial rennet, as most parmesan isn't vegetarian but there is a plethora of options out there!

PASTA WITH GRAPE TOMATOES AND BASIL

/ SERVES 4 / PREPARATION TIME 5 MIN. / COOKING TIME 15 MIN. /

 ## INGREDIENTS

1 pound dried pasta
¼ cup olive oil
3 garlic cloves, thinly sliced
3 oz. fresh basil, chopped
2 pints grape tomatoes
1 tsp Salt and pepper

 ## NUTRITION PER SERVING

CALORIES — 200   PROTEIN — 11.6   FIBER — 4.4
SUGARS — 1.3   FAT — 6.5

INSTRUCTIONS

1. In boiling salted water, cook the pasta until it gains a firmer texture.

2. Drain off and set it aside.

3. Meanwhile, in a large saucepan, heat oil over medium heat.

4. Add the garlic and cook for 1 minute while you stir occasionally. Add the grape tomatoes, basil, salt and pepper and cook for another 8 minutes while stirring occasionally.

5. Now, mix pasta with the sauce and stir well to serve warm.

MEDITERRANEAN BEETS WITH GARLIC AND OLIVE OIL

/ SERVES 4 / PREPARATION TIME 10 MIN. / COOKING TIME 1 HOUR

INGREDIENTS

2 pounds red beets, washed
2 garlic cloves, chopped
2 tbsp olive oil
a pinch of sea salt
a handful of cilantro, chopped

NUTRITION PER SERVING

CALORIES — 159   PROTEIN — 3.8   FIBER — 6.4
SUGARS — 1.7   FAT — 7.1

INSTRUCTIONS

1. Roast the beets by placing them on a baking sheet and roast in the oven at 400 F for nearly an hour or until it gets tender.

2. Place the beets in a pot to boil the beets. Pour in water and boil the water until you can pierce the beets easily with a fork.

3. Keep the beets in a baking dish to steam-roast the beets, pour in about quarter to half inch of water and wrap the baking dish with aluminium foil ensuring that the foil doesn't touch the beets.

4. Keep it in the oven and roast at 425F for next 1 hour or until tender.

TIP
While boiling beets, make sure you check the beets every once in a while because the water could evaporate during cooking, and end up exposing the top part of the beets.

ROASTED BEEF AND HORSE-RADISH WRAPS

/ SERVES 1 / PREPARATION TIME 15 MIN. / COOKING TIME 0 MIN. /

 ## INGREDIENTS

3 tbsp horseradish sauce
6 tbsp half-fat crème fraîche
2 large tortilla wraps
  Handful watercress
1 small red onion
4 slices cooked roast beef

 ## NUTRITION PER SERVING

CALORIES — 194   PROTEIN — 17   FIBER — 3
SUGARS — 2   FAT — 6

INSTRUCTIONS

1. Mix together 3 tbsp of horseradish sauce with 6 tbsp half-fat crème fraîche in a small bowl.

2. Drizzle and spread onto large tortilla wraps.

3. Distribute a few watercress in between each wrap together with a small red onion, finely sliced, and 4 slices cooked roast beef.

4. Cover each tortilla tightly and cut each in half and distribute in-between 2 plates.

5. Serve with the remaining horseradish crème fraîche, for dipping, and a handful lightly salted Kettle Chips.

CHICKEN GOATCHEESE QUESADILLAS

/ SERVES 2 / PREPARATION TIME 15 MIN. / COOKING TIME 10 MIN. /

INGREDIENTS

¾ oz. goat cheese, softened to room temperature
1 tbsp shredded Monterey jack cheese
¼ tsp virgin olive oil
2 tbsp chopped Vidalia onion
¼ cup frozen corn kernels, thawed
Pinch ground black pepper
¼ cup diced cooked skinless white-meat chicken
½ tbsp chopped fresh cilantro
2 six-inch corn tortillas

NUTRITION PER SERVING

CALORIES — 480   PROTEIN — 40   FIBER — 0
SUGARS — 2   FAT — 20

INSTRUCTIONS

1. Combine the cheeses in a medium bowl and keep it aside.

2. In a medium pan heat olive oil over the medium to low heat.

3. Mix together the onion and stir them for two minutes. Add the corn and pepper; sauté for one minute. Add the chicken and stir it for another one minute. Take it off the heat, and then stir in cilantro.

4. Evenly distribute the cheese mixture, and roll it over the couple of tortillas.

5. Layer each tortilla with half the chicken mixture, and season the remaining tortillas. Spray a large frying pan or griddle with cooking spray.

6. Slightly heat the quesadillas over medium heat for 5 minutes.

TOAST WITH CHEESE AND CINNAMON

/ SERVES 1 / PREPARATION TIME 5 MIN. / COOKING TIME 5 MIN. /

INGREDIENTS

2 cinnamon buns
1 small apple- peeled, cored and sliced
4 slices aged cheddar cheese
2 tbsp of butter
2 eggs
4 slices deli ham

NUTRITION PER SERVING

CALORIES — 123   PROTEIN — 2.4   FIBER — 2.5
SUGARS — 1.5   FAT — 5.1

INSTRUCTIONS

1. Distribute each of the buns in halves, and keep the slices on the kitchen surface to be worked on. To make a sandwich, keep the toppings in the same order as mentioned ahead: bottom of cinnamon bun, 1 slice cheddar cheese, 1 slice of brie cheese, apple slices, shredded ham, 1 slice of brie cheese, 1 slice of cheddar cheese, and top of cinnamon bun.

2. In a frying pan, melt the butter over medium heat level and swiftly mix together the eggs and milk in a bowl.

3. Dip both ends of the sandwich quickly into the egg mixture, frying the sandwiches until the colour becomes golden brown on either side spending about 2 minutes on each side.

GREEK PITA SALAD

/ SERVES 2 / PREPARATION TIME 15 MIN. / COOKING TIME 0 MINUTE

 ## INGREDIENTS

⅔	cup chopped seeded cucumber
⅔	cup chopped sweet red pepper
⅔	cup chopped tomato
⅔	cup chopped zucchini
¼	cup crumbled feta cheese
2	tbsp chopped ripe olives
2	tsp red wine vinegar
2	tsp lemon juice
¾	tsp dried oregano
⅛	tsp salt
⅛	tsp pepper
4	lettuce leaves
4	pita pocket halves

NUTRITION PER SERVING

| CALORIES — 350 | PROTEIN — 13 | FIBER — 7 |
| SUGARS — 1.7 | FAT — 20 | |

INSTRUCTIONS

1. Combine the cucumber, red pepper, tomato, zucchini, feta cheese and olives in a small bowl,
2. Mix together the vinegar, lemon juice, oregano, salt and pepper in another bowl.
3. Put over the vegetables and toss to coat.
4. Stuff the mixture into lettuce-lined pita halves.

Day 3 — Dinner

BURGER WITH MUSHROOM AND RADICCHIO

/ SERVES 1 / PREPARATION TIME 5 MIN. / COOKING TIME 5 MIN. /

INGREDIENTS

1	pound mixed exotic mushrooms, trimmed
¼	tsp kosher salt
¾	tsp freshly ground black pepper, divided
1¼	pounds ground sirloin
4	(2-ounce) whole-wheat hamburger buns split
1	small head radicchio, sliced into thin rings

NUTRITION PER SERVING

CALORIES — 450	PROTEIN — 38	FIBER — 5
SUGARS — 1.9	FAT — 20	

INSTRUCTIONS

1. Heat oil over medium-high heat in a large non-stick skillet. Add mushrooms and ¼ tsp of salt and pepper each, and cook while regularly stirring until it turns tender and golden in colour. Shift the mushrooms in a plate. Take out the skillet and reserve it for further use.

2. Turn the meat into 4 patties while sprinkling the remaining half-tsp pepper over either side of the burgers.

3. Come back to the skillet and heat over medium-high heat while cooking burgers for up to 6 minutes.

4. Start by placing one quarter of the radicchio slices, followed by the burgers, on bottom buns; divide mushrooms among burgers and top with other half of bun.

DAY 4

BOILED EGGS IN SETOCHKU

/ SERVES 1 / PREPARATION TIME 10 MIN. / COOKING TIME 15 MIN. /

INGREDIENTS

2 eggs
1½ tea spoon of reduced-fat sour cream
3 sliced grape tomatoes
1 slice turkey bacon
¼ cup cheddar cheese
½ ounce artichoke hearts
2 tsp finely chopped onions
10 inch flour tortilla
2 tsp prepared pesto sauce

NUTRITION PER SERVING

CALORIES — 400   PROTEIN — 16.2   FIBER — 0.3
SUGARS — 1.8   FAT — 25

INSTRUCTIONS

1. Break the eggs in a bowl. Blend it together with the sour cream and then stir it in the cheddar cheese.

2. Spray the cooking spray over the fry pan, and cook and stir the pesto sauce for the next 6 minutes over medium to high heat until the onion starts appearing translucent. Stir nicely and put in the tomatoes, and pour the egg mixture into the skillet.

3. Cook and stir the egg mixture until the eggs are thoroughly cooked but not dry, for about 2 ½ minutes. Once you have removed the eggs from the pan, set them aside.

4. Place one slice of the turkey bacon into the skillet, and let it fry, while flipping once, until the bacon is thoroughly cooked and begins to crisp and cream, cooking for about 3 minutes per side.

5. Finally, when the bacon is cooked, add the artichokes to the fry-pan and heat it for another 1 minute, and take the bacon and artichokes away from the pan.

6. Place the tortilla into the hot skillet Spray and drizzle the skillet with cooking spray. Heat the tortilla until it becomes warm and tender.

7. At the centre of the tortilla, spoon the eggs, turkey bacon, and artichokes and season them with salt and pepper. Fold the bottom 2 inches of the tortilla in order to enclose the filling, and wrap it firmly.

HEALTHY TURKEY WRAP

/ SERVES 1 / PREPARATION TIME 5-10 MIN. / COOKING TIME 5 MIN. /

INGREDIENTS

	Whole-wheat wrap
1	tbsp cranberry sauce
1	tsp cream cheese spread (light)
	Turkey zucchini ribbons
	Yellow squash ribbons
2-3	avocados
	Lettuce
	Handful of spinach
2	fresh tomatoes

NUTRITION PER SERVING

CALORIES — 371   PROTEIN — 0   FIBER — 0
SUGARS — 2   FAT — 15

INSTRUCTIONS

1. In a small bowl, combine the cranberry sauce and light cream cheese. Once it is thoroughly mixed together, spread on an entire whole-wheat tortilla.

2. Slice long strips from the zucchini with the help of a vegetable peeler, and place it in center of the tortilla.

3. Cut the avocado, lettuce, tomatoes, spinach, and turkey, and spread on tortilla.

4. Roll firmly with the cream cheese spread on the edges in order to seal it.

5. Let it cool down in fridge until you are ready to eat.

AVOCADO SALMON SALAD

/ SERVES 1 / PREPARATION TIME 5 MIN. / COOKING TIME 5 MIN. /

 ## INGREDIENTS

For salmon:
   Two (4-6 ounce) salmon fillets
1 tsp extra virgin olive oil
   Juice of 1 lemon
   Salt and pepper
For salad:
3-4 cups organic baby spinach
1 large pink grapefruit, peeled and sectioned
2 medium navel oranges, peeled and sectioned
1 avocado, thinly sliced
¼ to ½   cup sliced almonds
¼ cup green onions, sliced
   Juice of 1 lemon
2 tsp extra virgin olive oil
   Salt and pepper, to taste

NUTRITION PER SERVING

CALORIES — 309   PROTEIN — 28   FIBER — 9
SUGARS — 2.5   FAT — 14

INSTRUCTIONS

For salmon:

1. Heat the oven in advance at 425 degrees F.
2. Arrange a baking sheet together with parchment paper.
3. Keep the salmon fillets on baking sheet. Squeeze the fresh lemon over the salmon and sprinkle with a little olive oil.
4. Season well with salt and pepper as per you requirements.
5. Bake for the next 25 minutes, or until the salmon is completely cooked through.
6. Take it out from the oven and allow it to cool before you start assembling the salad.

For salad:

1. Keep the spinach in a bowl and top with citrus, avocado, and cooled salmon.
2. Shower the top with almonds and green onions.
3. Spray the fresh lemon juice over the top and drizzle with the olive oil. Season with salt and pepper as per your taste.

DAY 5
EGGS WITH TENDER BACON

/ SERVES 1 / PREPARATION TIME 5 MIN. / COOKING TIME 15 MIN. /

INGREDIENTS

2	lb. cubed potatoes
½	lb. bacon
1	sliced green bell pepper
1	red bell pepper
1	sliced onion
2	sliced cup mushrooms
1	salt, black pepper
3	cup cheddar cheese
8	eggs

NUTRITION PER SERVING

CALORIES — 136   PROTEIN — 9.2   FIBER — 9
SUGARS — 2   FAT — 10.49

INSTRUCTIONS

1. Boil water in a large pot. Add potatoes to it and cook until it tenders for 12-15 minutes.

2. Place the bacon in the large pan and cook it over even high heat until it turns brown. Cut it into small chunks and keep it aside.

3. Repeat the process with the potatoes until browned. Keep stirring regularly to prevent sticking.

4. Add in green bell pepper, red bell pepper, onion and mushroom and cook until they turn delicate. Cover the mixture with cheese and turn the mixture when the cheese melts.

5. Cook eggs to your liking and place potatoes in the large serving dish.

TIP
You could add flavour to the recipe by using potato toppers or try sour cream and onion or taco flavours.

STEWED RATATTOUILE WITH KALE

/ SERVES 1 / PREPARATION TIME 10 MIN. / COOKING TIME 35 MINUTE

INGREDIENTS

2 tbsp extra virgin olive oil
3 cloves of garlic
3 medium onions
1 spring fresh rosemary
1 tbsp rosemary dried
1 tbsp dried thyme
1 grape tomato pint
1 zucchini-small in size
1 red pepper
1 can of tomatoes
4 cups kale shredded
1 tsp salt

NUTRITION PER SERVING

CALORIES — 174.8   PROTEIN — 8.5   FIBER — 8
SUGARS — 2.3   FAT — 5

INSTRUCTIONS

1. Heat the oil in a medium pan over medium to high heat. Add the medium onions and garlic to the pan for 5-7 minutes until it turns light brown in colour.

2. Add the rosemary, thyme, tomatoes, zucchini, pepper, tomatoes, kale and salt to the pan.

3. Simmer the mixture for about 25 minutes while stirring it every 5 minutes.

BROWN RICE WITH TURKEY

/ SERVES 4 / PREPARATION TIME 15 MIN. / COOKING TIME 1 HOUR

INGREDIENTS

1⅓ cups dry short-grain brown rice
½ tsp kosher salt, divided
3 cups low-sodium chicken broth, divided
1 (2-pound) bone-in turkey breast
1 tsp olive oil
½ tsp freshly ground black pepper
1 tbsp low-sodium soy sauce, divided
4 cups baby spinach
1 bunch scallions, chopped
1 tbsp toasted sesame oil
1 tbsp toasted sesame seeds, optional

NUTRITION PER SERVING

CALORIES — 415   PROTEIN — 32.42   FIBER — 11.1
SUGARS — 3.1   FAT — 9.16

INSTRUCTIONS

1. Heat the oven in advance to 425°.

2. Mix together the rice, ¼ tsp salt, 2 cups of broth, and 1 cup water in a medium saucepan over medium heat, cover and boil the mixture. Decrease the heat to simmer and cook keeping it covered until the rice turns tender.

3. In the meantime, arrange a baking sheet with foil. Gently keep the turkey on sheet and cover it with oil. Season it with remaining one-quarter tsp salt and half-tsp pepper and brush with 1 ½ tsp soy sauce.

4. Roast until the turkey is cooked and the thermometer reads 165°, for about 55 minutes.

5. Take out of the oven transfer the turkey to a cutting board. Let it rest for a while and tent with foil.

6. Stir spinach, scallions, and the remaining 1 ½ tsp soy sauce into rice with the left over 1 cup warmed broth.

7. Thinly slice turkey and evenly distribute the rice and sliced turkey among 4 bowls sprinkle with sesame seeds to enjoy your meal.

VEGETABLES WITH LOW FAT CHEESE

/ SERVES 1 / PREPARATION TIME 10 MIN. / COOKING TIME 45 MIN. /

 ## INGREDIENTS

4 cups cauliflower florets
1 quartered mushroom 250 grams.
1 large red pepper
1 large yellow pepper
2 tbsp olive oil
1 tbsp salt
1 tbsp black pepper
3 tbsp low FAT cheese

 ## NUTRITION PER SERVING

CALORIES — 100   PROTEIN — 6.9   FIBER — 0
SUGARS — 1.4   FAT — 1.98

INSTRUCTIONS

1. Organize cauliflower florets and mushrooms in greased baking dish. Drizzle with a touch of oil. Sprinkle with salt and three kinds of pepper. Additionally toss lightly to finely coat.

2. Bake it properly in preheated 400 degrees F oven 25 minutes. Coat it well in pepper and garlic. Put it back in the oven. Bake for 20 minutes until vegetables are delicate.

3. Sprinkle lightly with cheese and low fat butter. Return to oven for a couple of minutes till cheese melt. You are ready to serve and enjoy the breakfast.

TIP
You could go the extra mile by trying the unique flavouring of the pasta sauce, like the ones complimented with the capers, wine and olives.

ROASTED CARROTS WITH LOW FAT PARMESAN CHEESE

/ SERVES 4 / PREPARATION TIME 15 MIN. / COOKING TIME 15 MIN. /

 ## INGREDIENTS

4 to **5** cups of carrots
¼ cup olive-oil
2 tsp minced garlic
2 tsp grated cheese
1-2 tsp panko bread crumbs
¾ tsp kosher salt to taste
¼ Tbsp black pepper to taste
Chopped parsley

 ## NUTRITION PER SERVING

CALORIES — 57   PROTEIN — 2.6   FIBER — 2.4
SUGARS — 0.5   FAT — 3.6

INSTRUCTIONS

1. Preheat oven to 350°F and line the baking sheet together with the foil. Grease it thoroughly with the non-stick cooking spray.

2. Arrange the olive oil, garlic, Parmesan, breadcrumbs, salt and pepper in a medium bag with a zip top. Add the carrots to it and then shake them thoroughly to get them nicely coated. You will then need to prad it out onto the prepared baking sheet.

3. Next, bake the contents for half an hour, while tossing with a spatula in the meantime.

4. Take out from the oven to serve.

TIP
The carrot may be cut smaller or baby carrots used,
which work wonders to decrease the total cooking time.
You could pre-cook the carrots half-way followed by roasting
the last half, which give the carrots a great and wonderful flavor!

Day 6 — Dinner

RED BEANS AND BROWN RICE WITH ASPARAGUS

/ SERVES 2 / PREPARATION TIME 10 MIN. / COOKING TIME 45 MIN. /

 INGREDIENTS

1   tsp olive oil
⅓ cup diced onion
1   crushed clove of garlic
½ cup diced celery
½ cup diced red pepper
½ cup diced yellow pepper
½ cup diced green pepper
¾ cup brown rice
1½ cups chicken stock
1   can drained red beans
½ tsp salt
    Fresh grounded pepper

 NUTRITION PER SERVING

CALORIES — 218.2   PROTEIN — 10.4   FIBER — 9.3
SUGARS — 3.4   FAT — 4.3

INSTRUCTIONS

1. Heat in a medium pan over medium-high heat, sauté onion & garlic in oil for couple of minutes until it becomes soft and tender.

2. Add celery and peppers and sauté for another 2 minutes.

3. Add dry rice and sauté for another 2 minutes.

4. Add chicken stock and beans and bring to a boil.

5. Reduce heat, cover and simmer 45 minutes.

6. Remove from heat and let it stand for at least 10 minutes.

7. Stir in salt and pepper.

TIP
The omelette's preparation consists of cubes of strips of meat cooked on skewers and served with spicy peanut sauce.

CREAM AND SOUP BROCCOLI

/ SERVES 8 / PREPARATION TIME 10 MIN. / COOKING TIME 40 MIN. /

INGREDIENTS

¼ cup (½ stick) unsalted butter
1 medium yellow onion, diced small
¼ cup all-purpose flour (spooned and levelled)
4 cups low-sodium chicken broth
1 pound broccoli, cut into florets,
  stems peeled and chopped
¼ cup heavy cream
  Coarse salt and ground pepper

NUTRITION PER SERVING

CALORIES — 206
SUGARS — 1,4

PROTEIN — 8.15
FAT — 11.9

FIBER — 2

INSTRUCTIONS

1. Melt butter in a medium pot, over medium heat.
2. Bring in the onion and cook while stirring occasionally until it becomes tender for about 8 minutes.
3. Bring in flour and cook while stirring occasionally till completely mixed, for about a minute.
4. Whisking regularly, bring in the broth and a cup of water to boil over the high heat. Decrease the heat and simmer, whipping occasionally for about 10 minutes.
5. Add broccoli and bring it to boil. Cook until broccoli becomes soft for about 20 minutes.
6. Shift the mixture to a large bowl. Fill a blender halfway in batches with mixture and puree until smooth; to help heat to escape, take off the cap from hole in lid, cover lid with a dish towel, and hold down firmly while blending. Put back the pureed soup into the pot.
7. Add the cream and cook over medium heat until it is thoroughly warmed.
8. Season with salt and pepper.

ROASTED GREEN BEANS AND RED PEPPER

/ SERVES 4-5 / PREPARATION TIME 10 MIN. / COOKING TIME 15 MINUTE

 INGREDIENTS

¾ pounds trimmed green beans
1 large stripped red bell pepper
1 tsp extra-virgin olive oil
     Salt and black ground pepper to taste

 NUTRITION PER SERVING

CALORIES — 88   PROTEIN — 4.6   FIBER — 5.2
SUGARS — 2.7   FAT — 0.7

INSTRUCTIONS

1. Heat the oven in advance to 600 degree F.
2. Mix together the green beans and red pepper with oil, salt and black ground pepper as per your requirement.
3. On a rimmed baking sheet, align in an even layer and roast all the ingredients at 600 degree F until it becomes tender or brown in colour, turning once halfway through cooking, about 10 minutes.
4. Once the vegetables have finished roasting, take them out from the oven and allow it to cool for about 5 minutes. Serve immediately garnished with the pistachios (crushed).

LENTILS, GARLIC WITH TOMATOES

/ SERVES 4 / PREPARATION TIME 5 MIN. / COOKING TIME 30 MIN. /

 ## INGREDIENTS

4 tsp olive oil
5 minced cloves of garlic
½ lb. Peeled and minced tomatoes
1 cup dried and washed lentils
1 tsp salt
1 tsp lemon juice

 ## NUTRITION PER SERVING

CALORIES — 210   PROTEIN — 13   FIBER — 7
SUGARS — 5   FAT — 11

INSTRUCTIONS

1. Heat the oil thoroughly in a medium 1 quart pot over medium to high heat.
2. Add garlic and cook until it becomes golden in colour.
3. Add tomatoes and cook until it becomes thick, for 8-10 minutes.
4. Add lentils together with 2 ½ glass of water.
5. Cover and reduce heat and bring to a boil.
6. Simmer the ingredients thoroughly for 20 minutes. Drain and transfer to the bowl. You are ready to eat it after getting it dressed with a combination of lemon juice, olive oil and pepper.

TIP
Toss the ingredients with the lemon dressing to keep things flavourful. Any kind of oil or vinegar based sauce or dressing that you have on hand could work wonders to add a different flavour!

CREAM AND SOUP OF ZUCCHINI

/ SERVES 4 / PREPARATION TIME 5 MIN. / COOKING TIME 15 MIN. /

INGREDIENTS

1 large diced green zucchini (about 2 cups)
1 small potato, peeled and diced
1 shallot, chopped
1 small clove garlic, chopped
1 tbsp (15 ml) olive oil
2 cups (500 ml) chicken broth
Plain yogurt
Chopped fresh chives
Salt and pepper

NUTRITION PER SERVING

CALORIES — 60   PROTEIN — 3   FIBER — 4
SUGARS — 3.5   FAT — 1

INSTRUCTIONS

1. In a small saucepan, soften the zucchini, potato, shallot and garlic in the oil. Season with salt and pepper.

2. Add the broth and bring to a boil. Cover and let the ingredients simmer for about 15 minutes or until the potatoes seem tender.

3. In a blender, purée the soup until it gets smooth. Adjust the seasoning as per your taste. Garnish with yogurt, drizzle with olive oil and sprinkle with fresh chives.

WHITE BEANS IN SPICY TOMATO SAUCE

/ SERVES 4 / PREPARATION TIME 10 MIN. / COOKING TIME 25 MINUTE

INGREDIENTS

1   tsp olive oil
2   cups diced gold potatoes
2   cloves minced garlic
¼   cup white wine, dry
1   cup cooked and drained navy beans
1   tsp paprika, smoked
1   tsp garlic powder
1   tsp onion powder
½   to **2** tsp red pepper flakes,
         crushed and garnished
         Handful of roasted lush red tomatoes
½   to **2** cup low-sodium vegetable's broth
1   tsp olive oil
½   cup shredded vegetarian parmesan
         Salt and black ground pepper to taste

NUTRITION PER SERVING

CALORIES — 99   PROTEIN — 6   FIBER — 5
SUGARS — 2   FAT — 2

INSTRUCTIONS

1. Heat carefully one 12 inch pan over medium to low heat. Add olive oil and whirl around the pan.

2. Add the potatoes to the pan and spread them out to make a fine layer. Cook until the potatoes are tender and could be easily removed from the pan (5 minutes).

3. Keep stirring and cooking potatoes for another 5 minutes or until the potatoes turn golden in colour and gets tender and delicate. Mix in the garlic and continue cooking for another minute to ensure that it is fragrant.

4. Pour in the white wine, in order to scrap up any potato stuck to the bottom. Then, add the white beans, smoked paprika, garlic powder, onion powder, and ½ tsp crushed red pepper.

5. Add the crushed tomatoes to the mixture and boil them to gradually reduce the heat from medium to low. Keep cooking until the sauce begins to gain thickness and the potatoes are softer than before (10 minutes).

6. Give the finishing touch to the dish with the combination of 1 tsp of the olive oil, parmesan, and salt to taste.

TIP
The potatoes will cook slowly once the tomato is added. To help them cook, add ¼ cup of the vegetable broth before adding the garlic. Cover and steam the potatoes until they get delicate.

MASHED POTATOES WITH GOAT CHEESE, ROSE-MARY AND OLIVE OIL

/ SERVES 4 / PREPARATION TIME 10 MIN. / COOKING TIME 30 MIN. /

INGREDIENTS

4	medium sweet potatoes
	Virgin olive oil
4	chopped cloves of garlic
2	sprig fresh rosemary leaves
	Salt and ground black pepper to taste
	Oz soft goat cheese (low fat)

NUTRITION PER SERVING

CALORIES — 238   PROTEIN — 7   FIBER — 5

SUGARS — 2   FAT — 6

INSTRUCTIONS

1. Boil the large pot stuffed with the salted water at medium to high heat. Merge together with the sweet potatoes and cook for 10-20 minutes till it becomes very tender.

2. As sweet potatoes cook, in the meantime heat 3 tbsp of the olive oil in a large frying pan over medium heat.

3. Add the garlic and rosemary while cooking for 10 minutes; keep stirring it frequently until it becomes very fragrant. Turn off heat, making sure that the garlic doesn't burn.

4. Once the sweet potatoes have finished cooking, shift them to a mixing bowl. Smash the recipe incorporating the back of a potato masher.

5. Use a spatula to scrape the olive oil, garlic and rosemary from the pan into the bowl while continuing to stir well. Add low fat goat cheese and pepper as per your requirements and let it cool down, to serve it.

TIP
If you wish to make the recipe ahead of time, cover the unbaked mashed potatoes' mixture tightly wrapped with foil and refrigerate no longer than 24 hours. Remove the cover and bake for up to 50 minutes.

CREAM SOUP OF SPINACH

/ SERVES 4-5 / PREPARATION TIME 10 MIN. / COOKING TIME 40 MIN. /

INGREDIENTS

1   medium onion
2   garlic cloves
1   medium potato
450 ml vegetable stock
500 ml low fat milk
500 g fresh spinach
     Freshly grated zest of half a lemon
     Freshly grated nutmeg
3   tbsp double cream

NUTRITION PER SERVING

CALORIES — 140   PROTEIN — 4   FIBER — 1
SUGARS — 1.7   FAT — 9

INSTRUCTIONS

1. Melt the butter in a saucepan; add the onion and garlic and fry gently for the next 6 minutes until it becomes tender.

2. Put in the potato and continue to cook gently for another 1 minute. Put in the stock and simmer for 10 minutes unless and until the potato begins to cook.

3. Pour in the milk and bring it to boil, and then stir in half the spinach and the lemon zest.

4. Keep it covered and continue to simmer for 15 minutes until the spinach has completely softened down. Let it cool for about 5 minutes.

5. Pour the soup into a blender and add the remaining spinach and process until it becomes silky and smooth.

6. Come back to the pan and heat it again.

7. Taste and season with salt, pepper and nutmeg as per your taste and requirement.

8. Serve the soup immediately after garnishing it with croutons.

TIP
The secret to the best soup is to cook half the spinach briefly in the soup to ensure depth of flavour, and then gradually add the remaining raw spinach during liquidising.

FISH STEW WITH POTATOES AND ONIONS

/ SERVES 1 / PREPARATION TIME 25 MIN. / COOKING TIME 1 HOUR

 ## INGREDIENTS

4	large garlic cloves cut in half with green shoots removed
4	anchovy fillets, soaked in water for 4 minutes, drained and rinsed
2	tbsp extra virgin olive oil
1	large onion, chopped
1	celery rib, chopped
1	medium carrot, chopped
	Salt, preferably kosher salt, to taste
1	can (28-ounce) chopped tomatoes, with liquid
1	quart water
1	pound small new potatoes, scrubbed and quartered or sliced
	A bouquet grain made with a bay leaf
	Freshly ground pepper
1	to **1½** pounds firm white-fleshed fish such as halibut, tilapia, Pacific cod or black cod, cut in 2-inch pieces.

NUTRITION PER SERVING

CALORIES — 169   PROTEIN — 20.64   FIBER — 2
SUGARS — 4.89   FAT — 3.3

INSTRUCTIONS

1. Keep the garlic cloves and quarter tsp salt in a mortar and pestle, and mash them to make a fine paste.

2. Add the anchovy fillets and mash it together with the garlic and then keep it to one side.

3. In a large soup pot or a Dutch made oven, heat the olive oil over medium to high heat and proceed to add the onion, celery and carrot with half a tsp of salt. Cook and stir until the onion becomes tender for about five minutes.

4. Add the pureed garlic and anchovy to the mixture while continuing to cook and stir until the mixture is very fragrant, for about one minute; finally proceed to mix the tomatoes.

5. Cook while stirring often, until the tomatoes have been cooked down and the mixture smells pleasing, for about 15 minutes.

6. Pour in the water, potatoes, salt the bouquet garni, and boil the mixture.

7. Decrease the heat to low, while covering the ingredients partially and boil it for half an hour. Adjust the salt and pepper according to your taste and take out the bouquet garni.

8. Season the fish with salt and pepper, and add it to the soup, once it has finished boiling.

9. Simmer for the next 10 minutes until it becomes tender.

10. Remove from the heat while stirring it in the parsley and serve immediately.

TIP
For milder seasoning, employ a can of diced tomatoes together with Italian herbs, such as basil, garlic and oregano.

SPAGHETTI WITH SHRIMP

/ SERVES 4 / PREPARATION TIME 5 MIN. / COOKING TIME 5 MIN. /

INGREDIENTS

8 oz. spaghetti
1 tbsp olive oil
2 cloves garlic, minced
4 oz. peeled and deveined shrimp
½ cup store-bought pasta sauce

NUTRITION PER SERVING

CALORIES — 300	PROTEIN — 20	FIBER — 8
SUGARS — 7	FAT — 2	

INSTRUCTIONS

1. Cook the pasta as per the instructions written on the package, using a heated up pot. Drain it and set aside

2. Heat the skillet up on a medium to high heat, and bring in the olive oil. Boil the garlic and add the shrimp.

3. Introduce the pasta sauce, reduce the heat and boil the mixture until the shrimp seems cooked and tender. Transfer the spaghetti into the skillet; stir well to mix it thoroughly.

4. Garnish with parsley and serve immediately.

TIP
You could choose your favorite olive variety for this recipe.
Additionally, a light fruity wine would complement this meal.

CREAM SOUP OF PUMPKIN AND POTATOES WITH SPICES

/ SERVES 5-6 / PREPARATION TIME 10 MIN. / COOKING TIME 35 MIN. /

INGREDIENTS

1	tbsp coriander seeds
1	clove garlic
2	tsp cumin seeds
2	tbsp olive oil
2	tsp dried oregano
1	sugar pumpkin
1	tbsp fennel seeds
4	sweet potatoes
½	tsp crushed red pepper
1	large onion, chopped
½	tbsp salt
1	quarts chicken broth
½	tsp whole black peppercorns

NUTRITION PER SERVING

CALORIES — 92.8   PROTEIN — 3.7   FIBER — 1.6
SUGARS — 3.1   FAT — 2.9

INSTRUCTIONS

1. In a large sauce pan, melt down the butter and boil onions and garlic until they get soft and do not stay any browner. Add the pumpkin and potatoes and cook for a few minutes, proceeding to add tomato paste, stock, seasonings, lemon juice and bring them to a boil.

2. Cover the pan while simmering it gently for the next half an hour or until they are tender. Puree the mixture in a blender and come back to a clean pan. Pour milk into the pan and bring it back to boil, whipping it continuously. Continue simmering it for another 2-3 minutes. Adjust seasonings as per your requirement and stir in sour cream.

3. Heat again and serve the soup sprinkled with coriander or parsley.

AUTUMN PUMPKIN MIX

/ SERVES 1 / PREPARATION TIME 10 MIN. / COOKING TIME 30 MIN. /

INGREDIENTS

¾ cup Brussels sprouts
1 cup cubed pumpkin
2 tsp olive oil
1 oz. crumbled goat cheese
2 tbsp pistachios
½ medium pear, sliced
2 tbsp balsamic vinegar
2 tsp yellow mustard

NUTRITION PER SERVING

CALORIES — 250   PROTEIN — 25   FIBER — 10
SUGARS — 1   FAT — 5

INSTRUCTIONS

1. Sprinkle the Pumpkin and the Brussels sprouts with oil while roasting them together, turning the oven half way through at 350°F, for nearly half an hour.

2. Take it out of the oven, and toss together with the remaining ingredients.

3. You are all set to serve the fresh and healthy, autumn pumpkin mix.

FRESH CORN SAUTE WITH RED PEPPER

/ SERVES 2 / PREPARATION TIME 5 MIN. / COOKING TIME 10 MIN. /

INGREDIENTS

2 tsp butter, preferably unsalted

2 cups of fresh corn kernels

¼ cup chopped green onions

¼ cup red bell pepper, nicely diced

¼ tsp salt

¼ tsp freshly ground black pepper to taste

NUTRITION PER SERVING

CALORIES — 85

PROTEIN — 3

FIBER — 2

SUGARS — 3.4

FAT — 2.9

INSTRUCTIONS

1. In a medium pan melt down the unsalted butter and boil it over medium to high heat.

2. Add the fresh corn kernels to the pan after boiling it for couple of minutes.

3. Proceed further by adding green onions, bell pepper, salt, and pepper to the pan; and bringing the mixture to a boil for another couple of minutes until it becomes crisp and soft. Adjust the red pepper seasoning as per your requirement.

4. Your dinner is ready to be served.

CONCLUSION

Congratulations! Whether you chose the 21 or 10-day meal plan, you have successfully completed a challenging but vitally important step in eradicating "bad" sugar from your diet and reintroducing healthy, whole foods containing "Good" sugar into your eating regime. At this point, your body has been running on clean, consistent and even energy for days on end. You are no longer relying on the "quick fix" of empty added sugar calories. Gone are those all too brief energy spikes and accompanying crashes, requiring more and even more "bad" sugar. You are feeling more rested, vigorous and happy and more than likely, eating and drinking less than you have in quite some time! Hopefully you have enjoyed the meals from the plans in this book, trying new foods and adding them to your favorites. The time you have spent preparing these healthy, balanced recipes has resulted in improved nutrition and energy, more than making up for so-called "convenience" foods that rob you of your health!

If you are in need of motivation to continue this healthy lifestyle, please take a moment and look at yourself in a mirror. Now think back to the person you were mere days or weeks ago: List the differences on a piece of paper and stick it on your refrigerator as visual inspiration should you feel like you miss some processed, sugary laden food from your past. Is it really worth it? Is there something you could do or accomplish or enjoy rather than backtracking and risking your health and well-being?

Remember, life is a work in progress. If you do occasionally give in to temptation or are fooled by a "Bad" sugar choice, simply chalk it up to experience and move on. Don't punish yourself by repeating the mistake. Reward yourself with a healthy, delicious whole food choice and celebrate your success!

FREE DOWNLOAD

YOUR FREE GIFT!
GET MORE FREE RECIPES IN 1 CLICK!

GET YOUR FREE RECIPES HERE:

www.frenchnumber.net/detox10

All information is intended only to help you cooperate with your doctor, in your efforts toward desirable weight levels and health. Only your doctor can determine what is right for you. In addition to regular check ups and medical supervision, from your doctor, before starting any other weight loss program, you should consult with your personal physician.

Disclaimer and Terms of Use: Effort has been made to ensure that the information in this book is accurate and complete, however, the author and the publisher do not warrant the accuracy of the information, text and graphics contained within the book due to the rapidly changing nature of science, research, known and unknown facts and internet. The Author and the publisher do not hold any responsibility for errors, omissions or contrary interpretation of the subject matter herein. This book is presented solely for motivational and informational purposes only.

Presented by French Number Publishing
French Number Publishing is an independent publishing house head-quartered in Paris, France with offices in North America, Europe, and Asia.
FNº is committed to connect the most promising writers to readers from all around the world. Together we aim to explore the most challenging issues on a large variety of topics that are of interest to the modern society.